1

FIRST
SPORTS
SOURCE

FIRST SOURCE TO

SOCCER

RULES, EQUIPMENT,
AND KEY PLAYING TIPS

by Danielle S. Hammelef

Consultant:
Crissy Makela
Varsity Soccer Coach
Mankato West High School
Mankato, Minnesota

CAPSTONE PRESS
a capstone imprint

First Facts are published by Capstone Press,
1710 Roe Crest Drive, North Mankato, Minnesota 56003
www.mycapstone.com

Library of Congress Cataloging-in-Publication Data
Cataloging-in-publication information is on file with the Library of Congress
Names: Hammelef, Danielle S., author.
Title: First Source to Soccer: Rules, Equipment, and Key Playing Tips /
By Danielle Hammelef.
Description: North Mankato, Minnesota : An imprint of Capstone Press, 2018. |
Series: First Facts. First Sports Source | Includes bibliographical references and index. |
Audience: Age 7-9. | Audience: K to Grade 3. Identifiers: LCCN 2016059569| ISBN 9781515769460
(library binding : alk.paper) | ISBN 9781515769484 (pbk. : alk. paper) | ISBN 9781515769507
(ebook pdf : alk. paper) Subjects: LCSH: Soccer—Juvenile literature.
Classification: LCC GV943.25 H34 2018 | DDC 796.334—dc23
LC record available at https://lccn.loc.gov/2016059569

Editorial Credits
Bradley Cole, editor; Sarah Bennett and Katy LaVigne, designers; Eric Gohl, media researcher;
Kathy McColley, production specialist

Photo Credits
Alamy Stock Photo: GPI Stock, 20 (left), imac, 21 (right); Dreamstime: G0r3cki, cover; iStockphoto:
strickke, 1, 17; Shutterstock: arx, 11, CosminIftode, 5, Dziurek, 19, liewluck, cover (background),
1 (background, middle), muzsy, 7, 20 (right), Pavel L Photo and Video, 9, v.schlichting, 21 (left),
Ververidis Vasilis, 15; SuperStock: Blend Images, 13

Design Elements: Shutterstock

Printed and bound in China.
004610

TABLE OF CONTENTS

INTRODUCTION Get in the Game! 4

CHAPTER 1 Ready to Play!. 6

CHAPTER 2 How the Game Works 12

CHAPTER 3 Rules of the Game 16

CHAPTER 4 Playing Tips 20

Glossary. 22

Read More. 23

Internet Sites. 23

Index 24

Get in the Game!

Imagine kicking a soccer ball into the net like Lionel Messi. Millions of people can't get enough of this action-packed game. What's better than watching soccer? Playing it. And you don't have to be a superstar like Lionel Messi or Carli Lloyd. Start learning the basic rules, and practice ball handling skills. Before you know it, you could be scoring your first goal.

"To see the ball and run after it, makes me the happiest man in the world."

–Diego Maradona, retired Argentina National Team Midfielder

FIFA WORLD CUP

The Fédération Internationale de Football Association (FIFA) World Cup is the world's greatest soccer tournament. Every four years countries compete to have the top soccer team in the world. Athletes play for their country instead of their regular professional teams. A different country hosts the World Cup tournament each time.

LIONEL MESSI

FACT
Soccer is one of the oldest sports in the world. More than 2,000 years ago the Chinese played Tsu' Chu. In this game players kicked a leather ball into a goal.

5

CHAPTER 1

Ready to Play!

Equipment

Soccer players don't use a lot of equipment. Their most important piece of gear is a soccer ball. Official game balls weigh 14 to 16 ounces (397 to 454 grams). Soccer **cleats** grip the field and make quick movements easier. Shin guards protect legs from kicks.

FACT
Goalkeepers wear protective gear. Padded gloves protect their hands and help them grip the ball.

cleat—a shoe with small tips on the bottom to help soccer players stop or turn quickly

The Playing Field

Soccer is played on a rectangular field of grass called a pitch. A center line divides the pitch in half. The **referee** places the ball in the middle of the center line to start play.

Goal lines frame both short ends of the field. Touchlines run along both longer sides. These lines show out-of-bounds and in-play areas.

FACT
Most soccer pitches are between 100 and 130 yards (90 to 120 meters) long. They are 50 to 100 yards (45 to 90 m) wide.

referee—a person who makes sure athletes follow the rules of a sport

Goal Areas

A goal stands at each end of the pitch. A net reaches between two goal posts on the sides. The top of the goal is the crossbar. A rectangular **penalty** area surrounds each goal. Inside each penalty area is a smaller goal box and a penalty spot. When the referee calls for a penalty kick, a player shoots from there.

A FLOATING PITCH

Believe it or not, soccer can be played on water. Marina Bay, Singapore, is home to the world's largest floating soccer pitch. The float measures 130 yards by 91 yards (120 m by 83 m). Six posts tie the steel landing to the sea floor.

penalty—punishment for breaking the rules of a game

Soccer Positions

Each team has 11 players on the field. A goalkeeper guards the goal and makes **saves**. The other 10 players are forwards, midfielders, or fullbacks. Most teams have two forwards, four midfielders, and four fullbacks.

Besides making saves, goalkeepers **clear** the ball far from the goal area. They watch the entire pitch and shout directions to their teammates.

FACT
Rogerio Ceni is a professional goalkeeper from Brazil. He holds the world record for the most goals scored by a goalkeeper with 131 goals.

save—a stopped shot

clear—to keep the ball far from the goal area by throwing or kicking it

Forwards score the most goals. They spend most of each game in the **opponent's** half of the field. Midfielders run the entire game. They switch between **offense** and **defense**. Fullbacks play defense and protect their goal. They are often the strongest players. Fullbacks try to take the ball away from the other team.

FACT
Midfielders are also called "mids," "middies," and "halfbacks." Two midfielders run up to 9.5 miles (15.3 kilometers) per game.

"Behind every kick of the ball there has to be thought."
–*Dennis Bergkamp, Netherlands National Team*

opponent—someone who competes against another in a game or contest
offense—the team that is in control of the ball and is trying to score
defense—the team that tries to stop the other team from scoring; the defense is the team that doesn't have the ball

CHAPTER 3

Rules of the Game

Professional soccer games have two 45-minute periods. A **kick-off** starts both halves. During the game, players try to score as many goals as they can. They also try to keep their opponents from getting the ball. Teams score goals by kicking or **heading** the ball into the goal. The team with the most goals at the end of the game wins.

"The only way to win is as a team."
–Pelé,
former Brazil National Team Forward
three-time World Cup champion

FACT
The referee only stops the game clock after the first half, for penalties, or if a player is injured.

kick-off—the kick that starts play
heading—to hit the ball with your head

Referees and Penalties

Referees call a **foul** if a player trips or pushes an opponent. When this happens the other team gets a **free kick**. Sometimes players are fouled inside the penalty area. Then they take a penalty kick from the penalty spot. The goalkeeper stays in the net. All the other players wait outside the penalty area until the player kicks the shot.

FACT

Only goalkeepers can touch the ball with their hands. Referees call fouls when other team members touch the ball with their hands.

foul—an action that is against the rules

free kick—a kick given to a team because the other team committed a foul

"True champions aren't always the ones that win, but those with the most guts."

—Mia Hamm,
former U.S. Olympian and
two-time World Cup winner

19

CHAPTER 4

Playing Tips

Now you know the basics of soccer. Use these tips to help you improve your game.

GOALKEEPING

Watch the ball all the way into your hands. Secure the ball by tucking it close to your chest. Wrap your hands and arms around it.

MIDFIELDING

Constantly check over both shoulders to see what is going on around you. Always know where the ball is. Keep an eye on the other players on the field.

DEFENDING

Stay low so you can **pivot** and quickly change direction. Shuffle backward, keeping your knees bent for balance. Stay on your toes for quick moves.

SHOOTING AND PASSING

When kicking, always point your non-kicking foot toward the target. Keep your eyes on the ball. Watch your kicking foot follow through the ball.

pivot—to turn only moving one leg

Glossary

clear (KLIHR)—to keep the ball far from the goal area by throwing or kicking it

cleat (KLEET)—a shoe with small tips on the bottom to help soccer players stop or turn quickly

defense (DEE-fenss)—the team that tries to stop the other team from scoring; the defense is the team that doesn't have the ball

foul (FOWL)—an action that is against the rules

free kick (FREE KIK)—a kick given to a team because the other team committed a foul

heading (HED-ing)—to hit the ball with your head

kick-off (KIK-off)—the kick that starts play

offense (AW-fenss)—the team that is in control of the ball and is trying to score

opponent (uh-POH-nuhnt)—someone who competes against another in a game or contest

penalty (PEN-uhl-tee)—punishment for breaking the rules of a game

pivot (PIV-uht)—to turn only moving one leg

referee (ref-uh-REE)—a person who makes sure athletes follow the rules of a sport

save (SAYV)—a stopped shot

Read More

Hurley, Michael. *Soccer*. Fantastic Sports Facts. Chicago: Raintree, 2013.

Lindeen, Mary. *Let's Play Soccer*. A Beginning to Read Book. Chicago: Norwood House Press, 2016.

Mattern, Joanne. *I Know Soccer*. I Know Sports. Ann Arbor, Mich.: Cherry Lake Publishing, 2014.

Internet Sites

FactHound offers a safe, fun way to find Internet sites related to this book. All of the sites on FactHound have been researched by our staff.

Here's all you do:
Visit www.facthound.com
Type in this code: 9781515769460

 Check out projects, games and lots more at
www.capstonekids.com

Index

Ceni, Rogerio, 12

cleats, 6

defense, 14, 21

field. *See* pitches

FIFA World Cup, 4, 16, 19

forwards, 12, 14

fullbacks, 12, 14

goalkeepers, 6, 12, 18, 20

goals, 4, 5, 10, 12, 14, 16

Lloyd, Carli, 4

Messi, Lionel, 4

midfielders, 4, 12, 14, 20

offense, 14

penalties, 10, 11, 16, 18

pitches, 6, 8, 10, 11, 12, 14, 20

referees, 8, 10, 16, 18

shin guards, 6